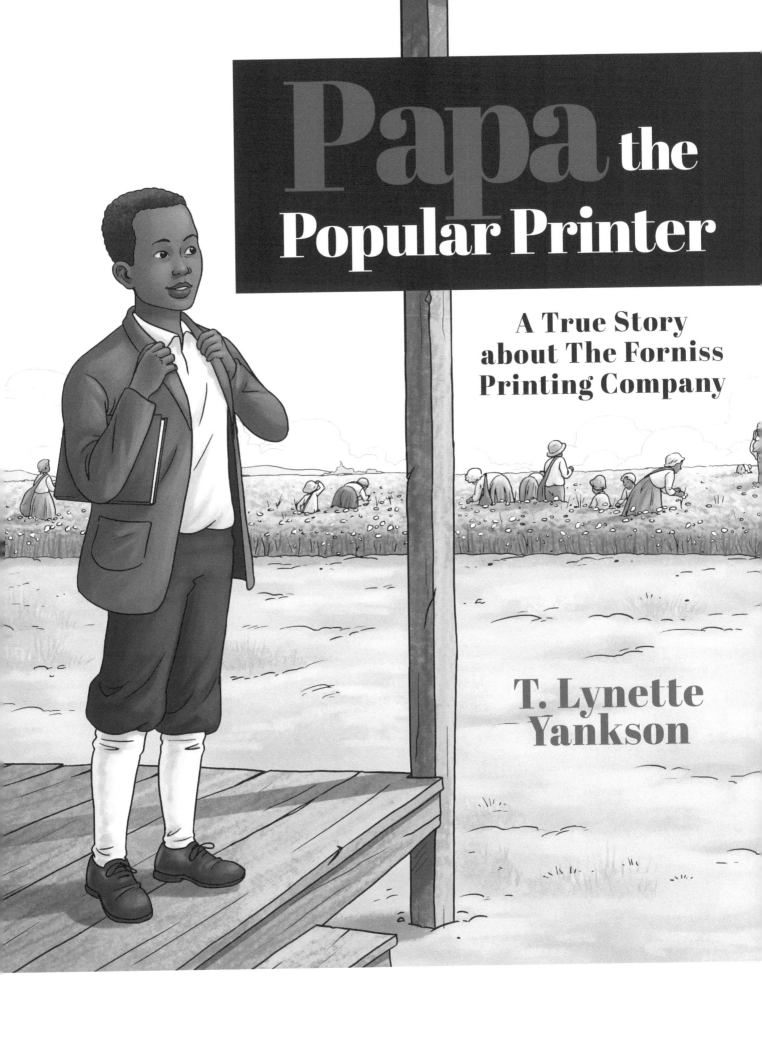

Papa the Popular Printer

the

A True Story about The Forniss Printing Company

T. Lynette Yankson

ISBN: 979-8-89109-170-2 - paperback
ISBN: 979-8-89109-171-9 - ebook

This Book Belongs To:

_____

Dedication

In dedication and loving memory of James Henry Forniss, my maternal grandfather. May your "extraordinary" true life story of perseverance and faith inspire others to exert efforts to actively advance humanity.

In loving memory of Thomas and Thelma Prince my parents and educators who instilled in me courage and faith to realize my dreams.

To my son, the light of my life, my loving daughter-in-law, and beautiful brilliant grandchildren. Sincere gratitude to all supportive family members and friends.

To my Infinite Wisdom Seekers (IWS) Book Club members whose years of valuable friendships and dialogues have mystically enhanced our human revolution or inner change and inspired me to also become an author.

To every reader who's determined, encouraged, and focused on accomplishing their dreams to manifest their unique life's mission.

To myself, for persevering and finishing a book I hope inspires others to also achieve their goals.

To the vast majority among us, who strive to rise up against adversity, stand up for justice, strive for peace and respect for ALL humanity.

James Henry Forniss, whom everyone called "JH", was born November 19, 1883 in Wilcox County, Alabama to Jane and Robert Forniss. His parents were born during slavery. Fortunately, they were not enslaved. Respecting post slavery conduct, his parents

taught their children to have faith, be humble, respectful and to know they too are equal to everyone else.

JH was a bright eyed, adventurous, skinny little "colored" boy who was excited to wake up early, get dressed, eat breakfast and be ready

in time to go to school. He knew going to school was important and a
privilege. Some children had to work in the fields picking cotton, while
others worked as sharecroppers to survive and could not go to school.

Some days he would leave early and walk to school alone, thinking of what new book he would discover at the school library. He thought, "today I'll read a book about the invention of the automobile!" When walking to school with friends, he enjoyed quizzing them on lessons they learned to encourage his peers.

After school and on weekends, he played games with other children. They enjoyed playing tag, hide and seek, shooting marbles, baseball and basketball. Children played freely in grassy fields and on bumpy roads made out of dirt and gravel.

One day, curious JH was walking in town; he kept peeking through the windows of the Canebrake Herald Printing Office. The owner Mr. White, came to the door and shouted

"HEY BOY STOP!" Why are you peeking your big nose in my printing office windows?" JH was shocked but replied kindly, "Sir, I'm sorry, I've never seen a printing shop, it sure looks interesting!" Mr. White thought,

"I've never noticed children peeking in the windows before". He said,
"You seem like a nice boy, what is your name?" "Sir, my name is James
Henry Forniss, but people call me JH!" "Sir what is your name please?"

"I'm Mr. White!" Hey boy, I know your daddy, Robert Forniss; you come from a "good colored family". "How old are you and do you go to school?" "Sir, I'm 12 years old and I finished the sixth grade. I don't go to school now because I must help my mother with my siblings and house chores."

"Well, can you read?" "Yes sir, but I want to learn to read better."
"Do you work boy? Yes sir, I work on my family's farm, feeding the chickens, slopping the hogs and watering our garden."

"Well boy, you get on back home and do not come peeking in my printing office windows again!!" JH was sad because he was so curious about how all those machines worked at the printing office.

JH thought, "oh well, I guess I'll never see what's inside of a printing shop." That night JH dreamt a big blue monster was chasing him, but he ran and hid and the monster ran the other way. He woke up thinking "wow, that dream was about Mr. White!"

JH told his good friends about what happened with Mr, White. The week after, JH walked to town, making sure he did not walk on the side of the street of the printing office. He did not even

look across the street towards the shop because he was still angry that Mr. White told him not to ever come back to his printing office. JH prayed daily for strong faith and courage to overcome his anger

at Mr. White. A few weeks later, JH and friends walked to town. This time JH felt confident and wasn't worried about Mr. White anymore, so he walked right by the printing office. Mr. White ran outside and

called out, "Hey JH, how have you been? I was wondering, would you be willing to work in my printing office?" JH was surprised, "I think so but I don't know how to be a printer." "NO not as a printer but

as a shoe shiner." "A shoe shiner?" "Yes, do you know how to shine shoes?" "Yes sir, I sure do!" "OK, the job is yours!" "Can you start tomorrow, 9am sharp?" "Yes and thank you Mr White!" JH was happy as

his prayers were answered. He reported to work on time everyday and always did his best, like his parents taught him. Soon, word spread that JH was the best shoe shiner in town and he brought more business to the

printing office. Due to his great work ethic, Mr. White appointed JH as his apprentice in training. JH was quickly learning how to operate the Remington manual typewriter, typesetting, the printing press and even the printing telegraph. A few years later,

Mr. White appointed JH as the Head Manager of the Canebrake Herald Printing Office! Walking home from work one evening, JH stopped to talk to his neighbor. A beautiful young lady named Annie Julia Jones was walking by and his neighbor introduced her to JH.

James and Annie became friends and enjoyed each other's company. After courting for one year, they fell in love and he asked Annie to marry him. She happily said "YES" and they soon married! James was 20 years

old and Annie 19. A few years later, Mr. White became sickly and left the printing business in the hands of JH. By the time JH reached his 30's; The Forniss Printing Company of Uniontown, AL was established!!

JH became the editor of a popular newspaper known as the "Uniontown News". In 1909, JH founded The Negro Leader newspaper that became highly popular too. Many considered JH first class in his profession as a printer. As JH matured, he realized Uniontown, AL

was growing and in need of various civic services. In order
to support the residents of Uniontown, AL; JH became a
Notary Public to assist with certification of legal documents.
A member of the Uniontown school board to help advance

education of the youth. JH was a Deacon of the Quinn Chapel AME Church and actively involved in many leadership roles. So faithful to his duties, his church sent him as a representative to the electoral college conference, where he

was elected as a lay delegate to the Centennial General Conference held in Philadelphia May 1916.

Likely, everyone in Uniontown, AL in the early 1900's knew JH Forniss. His stature was lean standing a towering six feet tall. Most everyone

with common "southern hospitality" was friendly. When passing by, they would smile and nod greeting him "Hey JH" or "Hey Mr. Forniss". As an elder, his children, grandchildren and relatives affectionately called him "PAPA FORNISS!" He was loved by many. As the local

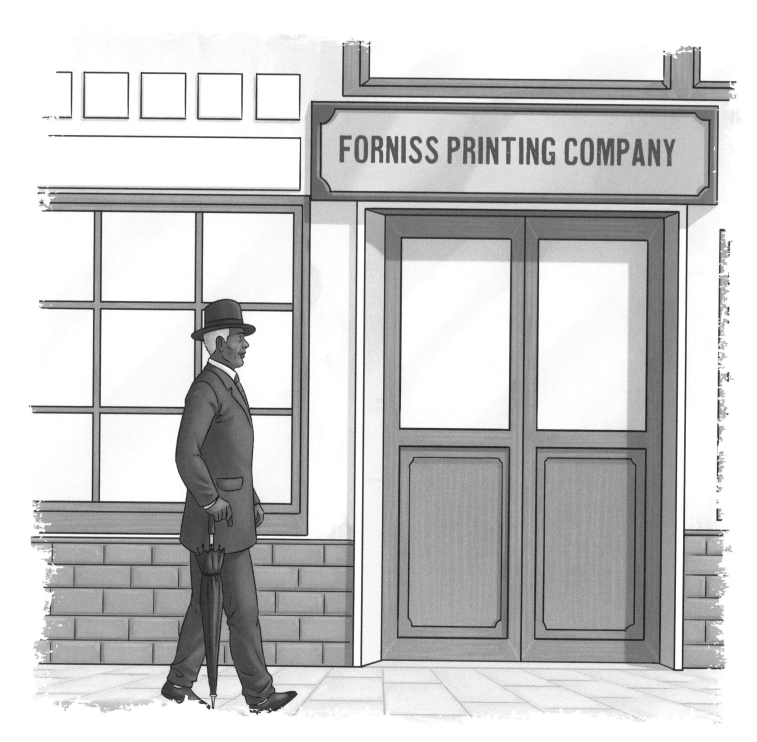

story goes; "JH would wear a nice three-piece suit, hat and his gold pocket watch every morning and walk to town to The Forniss Printing Company carrying his umbrella come rain or shine!" JH was determined as he struggled against all

odds, especially for colored people[1]; to be a Community Activist in the early 20th Century post slavery era. He was keenly aware that by supporting his hometown's development and building a strong foundation that the citizens of Uniontown, AL would lead a higher quality life.

---

[1] "Colored People" a racial descriptor historically used in the United States during the Jim Crow law 1877-1954.

To the marriage of JH and Annie, six children were born; four girls and two boys. Millard Forniss, his second son, was his apprentice for many years. After learning the printing business, he and his

FORNISS PRINTING COMPANY BIRMINGHAM, AL

family moved north to later establish the Forniss Printing Company in downtown Birmingham, AL in the late 1930's. Currently, there's a street in Uniontown named in honor of Mr. James Henry Forniss. The street sign, "W. Forniss", stands today about two blocks from

where his home was located. If you ever visit Uniontown, AL, please find the street and take a picture standing by the street sign! James Henry Forniss died October 17, 1972 at 89.

Papa Forniss' life is a great lesson on living a faithful life and being of service to people. With Faith, Persistence and Hard Work, ALL THINGS ARE POSSIBLE! THE END!

40

About The Author

T. Lynette Yankson was born and raised in Detroit, MI during the turbulent 1960's and 70's. She lived in Atlanta, GA, the "Black Mecca of the South" from 1980 until 2019. She currently resides in North Carolina, thrilled to be near her loving family, especially engaging with her "beautiful, brilliant" grandchildren! She enjoys conversing, encouraging, and learning from the bright minds of youths. Her faith, family, friends and health are of utmost importance.

Growing up in northern urban America, her family looked forward to traveling south annually to visit her loving relatives in Alabama. Experiencing "life in the south" was a dramatically different lifestyle; "a culture shock". She enjoyed visits with the Prince's, her paternal grandparents and relatives. However, most visits were with her maternal grandfather James Henry

Forniss aka "Papa Forniss" in his elder 80"s. Her mother, Thelma L. Forniss-Prince; would faithfully walk her around her beloved hometown of Uniontown, AL with pride to meet and greet relatives, friends and business owners. As a young girl, she was intrigued when walking by the "remnants" of Papa Forniss' print shop the "Forniss Printing Company". That experience left an indelible impression engraved in her heart and memory.

She earned a Bachelors of Business Administration in Marketing from Eastern Michigan University in 1980. She enjoyed her career as a Civilian Service Procurement Systems Analyst and technical report writer. Upon retirement, she received a Letter of Commendation from President Barack Obama in 2015.

Inspired by her passionate interest in natural health and healing, she studied at Ahimki Center for Wholeness under mentor Dr. Mark Armstrong. In 2006, she attained a Master's of Holistic Theology.

Book Description

"Papa the Popular Printer" is an extraordinary nonfiction story about protagonist James Henry Forniss, aka JH and Papa Forniss. He evolves from a young man as a shoe shiner, to become a successful Professional Printer, akin to today's Information Technologist or "IT" person. His ingenious transformation was rare, especially for a "colored man" in the south during post slavery 20th Century era.

A true story of growing up in America as a "Colored or Negro" person overcoming challenges of racial barriers in the early 1900's. Children will learn about "The Power of One". Youth will be inspired by how JH's stand alone faith, confidence and courageous actions to "never give up" changed his life. As a catalyst for change, JH became a Community Activist whose influence dramatically enhanced the development of Uniontown, AL.

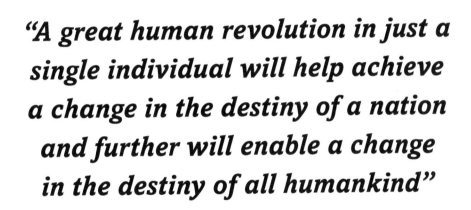

"A great human revolution in just a single individual will help achieve a change in the destiny of a nation and further will enable a change in the destiny of all humankind"

—Daisaku Ikeda

PAPA THE POPULAR PRINTER

R	N	E	G	R	O	L	E	A	D	E	R	S	N
G	F	O	R	N	I	S	S	E	D	I	T	O	R
U	N	I	O	N	T	O	W	N	N	E	W	S	E
P	T	I	R	E	C	R	T	C	H	T	I	A	F
S	R	A	E	C	N	E	D	I	F	N	O	C	T
C	W	A	E	R	E	T	I	R	W	E	P	Y	T
I	R	L	Y	I	P	Y	O	I	I	R	R	R	A
H	N	O	G	E	R	C	E	D	E	N	I	T	C
T	I	A	N	E	R	A	O	Y	N	H	N	P	T
E	S	A	S	O	P	S	I	U	O	F	T	W	I
K	T	R	N	D	E	E	I	N	R	E	E	E	V
R	N	E	W	S	P	A	P	E	R	A	R	N	I
O	T	P	E	T	A	G	E	L	E	D	G	F	S
W	E	C	N	E	T	S	I	S	R	E	P	E	T

FORNISS
FAITH
PRINTER
NEGRO LEADER
PRAYERS
UNIONTOWN NEWS
COURAGE
DELEGATE
WORK ETHICS
CONFIDENCE
EDITOR
TYPEWRITER
NEWSPAPER
PERSISTENCE
ACTIVIST

Printed in the USA
CPSIA information can be obtained
at www.ICGtesting.com
CBHW070200090224
4193CB00013B/110